MINOR YOGA UPANISHADS

English Translation Accompanied by Sanskrit Text in Roman Transliteration

Swami Vishnuswaroop

Divine Yoga Institute
Kathmandu, Nepal

DEDICATION

Tasmai Shri Gurave Namah!
This book is dedicated to my Guru
Swami Satyananda Saraswati,
Founder of Bihar School of Yoga,
Munger, India.

-Swami Vishnuswaroop

CONTENTS

INTRODUCTION

This text "Minor Yoga *Upanishads*" is a collection of five small Yoga *Upanishads*. They are *Amritanada, Amritavindu, Kshurika, Yogaraja*, and *Hamsa Upanishads* respectively. Even though they are small *Upanishads* in textual length and size, they contain and impart profound philosophical, theoretical and practical knowledge and wisdom on various branches and aspects of yoga. Anyone who wishes to have a quick insight into the *Vedantic* view of yoga, then these *Upanishads* briefly provide all information that is necessary to be understood, followed, and practiced in a proper way in order to achieve the ultimate spiritual goal of human life.

It is hoped that English translation of Sanskrit text accompanied by Roman transliteration will be helpful and beneficial to all readers. A key to transliteration is given at the end of the text.

Publisher

AMṚTANĀDA UPANIṢAD

अमृतनाद उपनिषद्

Book One

English Translation Accompanied by Sanskrit Text in Roman Transliteration

Translated into English by
Swami Vishnuswaroop

Divine Yoga Institute
Kathmandu, Nepal

INTRODUCTION

Amṛtanāda Upaniṣad belongs to *Kriṣna Yajurveda*. In this *Upaniṣad* meditation on OM (*Oṅkāra*) along with the six limbs of yoga - *pratyāhāra* (withdrawal of senses), *dhyāna* (meditation), *prāṇāyāma* (restraint of breath), *dhāraṇā* (concentration), *tarka* (discussion, reflection in agreement with the *śāstras* i.e. *Vedas* and *samādhi* are described. Techniques of *prāṇāyāma,* meditation on the various *mātrās* of OM and the regions of five *prāṇas* and their colors are described. A *sādhaka* is guided on how to get rid of fear, anger and hatred. Instructions are given on food and drinks, action and rest, and sleeping and waking to maintain a good balance in life and finally, how to attain a divine life leading to *mośha* (liberation). Thus, the major subjects of yoga with its ultimate goal are presented in this *Upaniṣad.*

In order to make this text more readable Sanskrit verses are given in Devnagari along with their Roman transliteration. A key to trasliteration is given at the end of the text. It is hoped that this collection of Minor Yoga *Upaniṣads* will be helpful for all who are interested to have the *Vedāntic* view on various aspects of yoga.

Publisher

ŚĀNTIPĀṬHAḤ

शान्तिपाठः

ॐ सह नाववतु ।

सह नौ भुनक्तु ।

सह वीर्यं करवावहै ।

तेजस्विनावधीतमस्तु मा विद्विषावहै ॥

ॐ शान्तिः शान्तिः शान्तिः ॥

oṃ saha nāvavatu /

saha nau bhunaktu /

saha vīryaṃ karavāvahai /

tejasvināvadhītamastu mā vidviṣāvahai /

oṃ śāntiḥ śāntiḥ śāntiḥ //

Om. May He protect both of us together. May He nourish both of us together. May both of us get strength and power together. May our knowledge (given and received between us) be powerful. May there be no animosity between us. Om. May there be peace, peace and peace again in all the three worlds. May the three types of pains/miseries be peaceful.

BOOK ONE

Amritanada Upanishad

अमृतनाद उपनिषद्

Goal of Human Life

शास्त्राण्यधीत्य मेधावी अभ्यस्य च पुनः पुनः ।

परमं ब्रह्म विज्ञाय उल्कावत्तान्यथोत्सृजेत् ॥१॥

śāstrāṇyadhītya medhāvī abhyasya ca punaḥ punaḥ /

paramaṃ brahma vijñāya ulkāvattānyathotsṛjet //1//

The highly intelligent one, after studying all the *śāstras* (scriptures) and practicing them repeatedly, should realize the knowledge of the *Brahma*. As this life is transient like the light of a meteor, he should raise him (above the cycle of worldly existence). -1.

Worship of Rudra

ओङ्काररथमारुह्य विष्णुं कृत्वाथ सारथिम् ।

ब्रह्मलोकपदान्वेषी रुद्राराधनतत्परः ॥२॥

oṅkārarathamāruhya viṣṇuṃ kṛtvātha sārathim /

brahmalokapadānveṣī rudrārādhanatatparaḥ //2//

Having mounted on the chariot of *Oṅkāra* (OM) and befriended with Lord *Viṣṇu* as his charioteer, one who wishes to reach the seat of *Brahmaloka* should attentively engage in the worship of *Rudra*. -2.

Oṅkāra Leads to the Supreme

तावद्रथेन गन्तव्यं यावद्रथपथि स्थितः ।

स्थित्वा रथपतिस्थानं रथमुत्सृज्य गच्छति ॥३॥

tāvadrathena gantavyaṃ yāvadrathapathi sthitaḥ /

sthātvā rathapatisthānaṃ rathamutsṛjya gacchati //3//

As long as one should go by the chariot (in the form of *Oṅkāra*) until the path that can lead ahead is completed. Having reached the place of the lord of the chariot, then giving up the chariot he departs his own way. -3.

Meditation on the Īśvara

मात्रालिङ्गपदं त्यक्त्वा शब्दव्यञ्जनवर्जितम् ।

अस्वरेण मकारेण पदं सूक्ष्मं हि गच्छति ॥४॥

mātrāliṅgapadaṃ tyāktvā sabdavyañjanavarjitam /

asvareṇa makāreṇa padam sūkṣmaṃ hi gacchati //4//

Having given up the *mātrā* (*akāra,* etc,) *liṅga* (mark, characteristic) and *pada* (the word) of *praṇava,* (meditating on the *Īśvara*) in the form of *makāra* (the alphabet 'M') without any *svara* (accent), he enters into *sūkṣma pada* (the subtle seat). -4.

Practice of Pratyāhāra

शब्दादि विषयान्पञ्च मनश्चैवातिचञ्चलम् ।

चिन्तयेदात्मनो रश्मीन्प्रत्याहारः स उच्यते ॥५॥

śabdādi viṣayānpañca manaścaivāticañcalam /

cintayedātmano raśmīnpratyāhāraḥ saḥ ucyate //5//

The five objects sound, touch, sight, taste and smell, and their respective receiving senses and the highly unstable mind should be seen as the rays of *Ātmā* like the sun (the mind and senses exists due to the light of *Ātmā* alone). Such reflection of *Ātmā* is called *pratyāhāra.* -5.

Six Limbs of Yoga

प्रत्याहारस्तथा ध्यानं प्राणायामोऽथ धारणा ।

तर्कश्चैव समाधिश्च षडङ्गो योग उच्यते ॥६॥

pratyāhārastathā dhyānaṃ prāṇāyāmo'tha dhāraṇā /

tarkaścaiva samādhiśca ṣaḍaṅgo yoga uchyate //6//

Pratyāhāra (withdrawal of senses), *dhyāna* (meditation), *prāṇāyāma* (restraint of breath), *dhāraṇā* (concentration), *tarka* (reflection, discussion in agreement with the *śāstras*), *samādhi* are called the six limbs of yoga. -6.

Prāṇa Purifies Indriyas

यथा पर्वतधातूनां दह्यन्ते धमनान्मलाः ।

तथेन्द्रियकृता दोषा दह्यन्ते प्राणधारणात् ॥७॥

yathā parvatadhātūnāṃ dahyante dhamanānmalāḥ /

tathaindriyakṛtā doṣā dahyante prāṇadhāraṇāt //7//

Just like the impurities of the mountain-ores (gold, iron, etc.) are burnt off by the blower, so the impurities generated by *indriyas* (the senses) are destroyed by the restraint of *prāṇa* (the breath). -7.

Dhāraṇā Purifies All Sins

प्राणायामैर्दहेद्दोषान्धारणाभिश्च किल्बिषम् ।

प्रत्याहारेण संसर्गान् ध्यानेनानीश्वरान्गुणान् ॥८॥

किल्बिषं हि क्षयं नीत्वा रुचिरं चैव चिन्तयेत् ॥९॥

prāṇāyāmairdaheddoṣāndhāraṇābhiśca kilbiṣam /

pratyāhāreṇa saṃsargān dhyānenānīśvarānguṇān //8//

kilbiṣaṃ hi kṣayaṃ nītvā ruciraṃ caiva cintayet//9//

The (store of) impurities (of the senses) should be burnt by *prāṇāyāma* and the sins by *dhāraṇā*. All the faults arising from the association (of the worldly objects) should be destroyed by *pratyāhāra* and the atheistic qualities by *dhyāna*. In this way, having certainly destroyed all sins and impurities, one should verily contemplate on *Rucira* (the pleasant form of his deity). -8-9.

Three Prāṇāyāmas

रुचिरं रेचकं चैव वायोराकर्षणं तथा ।

प्राणायामस्त्रयः प्रोक्ता रेचपूरककुम्भकाः ॥१०॥

ruciraṃ recakaṃ caiva vāyorākarṣaṇaṃ tathā /

prāṇāyāmastraya proktā recapūrakakumbhakā //10//

In this way, retaining the *prāṇa* within by contemplating on the attractive form (of the deity) is *kumbhaka*, exhaling the breath is *recaka* and inhaling the breath is *pūraka*. Thus, the three types of *prāṇāyāma* are called *recaka, pūraka* and *kumbhaka*. -10.

Practice of Gāyatri Mantra

सव्याहृतिं सप्रणवां गायत्रीं शिरसा सह ।

त्रिः पठेदायतप्राणः प्राणायामः स उच्यते ॥११॥

savyāhṛtiṃ sapraṇavāṃ gāyatriṃ śirasā saha /

triḥ paṭhedāyataprāṇaḥ prāṇāyāmaḥ sa ucyate //11//

A *sādhaka* should practice extended *prāṇāyāma* (*pūraka, kumbhaka* and *recaka*) along with the (mental) repetition of *gāyatri* mantra three times (a day) with its *vyāhṛtis, praṇava* and *śira* (head). This way of practice is called *prāṇāyāma*. -11.

Sign of Recaka

उत्क्षिप्य वायुमाकाशे शून्यं कृत्वा निरात्मकम् ।

शून्यभावेन युञ्जीयाद्रेचकस्येति लक्षणम् ॥१२॥

utkṣipya vāyumākāśe śūnyaṃ kṛtvā nirātmakam /

śūnyabhāve niyuñjīyādrecakasyeti lakṣaṇam //12//

Expelling the *vāyu* in the sky and making the heart region devoid of air one should make his mind stable in void without any thoughts. This is the sign of *recaka* (*prāṇāyāma*). -12.

Sign of Pūraka

वक्त्रेणोत्पलनालेन तोयमाकर्षयेन्नरः ।

एवं वायुर्ग्रहीतव्यः पूरकस्येति लक्षणम् ॥१३॥

vaktreṇotpalanālena toyamākarṣayennaraḥ /

evaṃ vāyurgrahītavyaḥ pūrakasyeti lakṣaṇam //13//

Just like a man draws water into his mouth with the stalk of a lotus, similarly inhaling *prāṇa vāyu* slowly (and gently) is the sign of *pūraka* (*prāṇāyāma*). -13.

Sign of Kumbhaka

नोच्छ्वसेन्न च निश्वसेन्नैव गात्राणि चालयेत् ।

एवं भावं नियुञ्जीयात्कुम्भकस्येति लक्षणम् ॥१४॥

nocchvasenna na ca niśvasennaiva gātrāṇi cālayet /

evam bhāvaṃ niyuñjīyātkumbhakasyeti laksaṇam //14//

Neither there is inhalation nor exhalation nor the body is moving. In this way, remaining in a steady state (of the body, *prāṇa* and mind) is the sign of *kumbhaka* (*prāṇāyāma*). -14.

Sign of Tranquility

अन्धवत्पश्य रूपाणि शब्दं बधिरवच्छृणु ।

काष्ठवत्पश्य वै देहं प्रशान्तस्येति लक्षणम् ॥१५॥

andhavatpaśya rūpāṇi śabdaṃ badhiravacchṛṇu /

kāṣṭhavatpaśya vai dehaṃ praśāntasyeti laksaṇam //15//

One should see all names and forms (in the objective world) like a blind, hear sound like a deaf and see the body like a wood. This is the sign of tranquility (of a person). -16.

Practice of Dhāraṇā

मनःसङ्कल्पकं ध्यात्वा संक्षिप्यात्मनि बुद्धिमान् ।

धारयित्वा तथात्मानं धारणा परिकीर्तिता ॥१६॥

manaḥsaṅkalpakaṃ dhyātvā saṅkṣipyātmani buddhimān /

dhārayitvā tathātmānaṃ dhāraṇā prakīrtitā //16//

A wise *Sādhaka* should know that the mind is *saṅkalpaka* (desiring) and should dissolve it into his *Ātmā* (pure intelligence). Then the pure intelligence in the form of *Ātmā* should be established in the contemplation of *paramātman.* This state of contemplation is called *dhāraṇā*. -16.

Right Tarka (Reasoning)

आगमस्याविरोधेन ऊहनं तर्क उच्यते ।

समं मन्येत यल्लब्ध्वा स समाधिः प्रकीर्तितः ॥१७॥

āgamasyāvirodhena ūhanaṃ tarka ucyate /

samaṃ manyeta yallabdhvā sa samādhiḥ prakīrtitaḥ //17//

Speculation or reasoning in agreement with *āgama* (*vedas*) is called *tarka.* When all worldly objects are regarded as mean or baseless through the attainment of the right *tarka* (reasoning), then this state of mind is called the state of *samādhi*. -17.

Oṅkāra Sādhanā

भूमौ दर्भासने रम्ये सर्वदोषविवर्जिते ।

कृत्वा मनोमयीं रक्षां जप्त्वा वै रथमण्डले ॥१८॥

bhūmau darbhāsane ramye sarvadoṣavivarjite /

kṛtvā manomayiṃ rakṣāṃ japtvā vai rathamaṇḍale //18//

Keeping the ground clean in a pleasant area free from all kinds of faults (impure things, insects, reptiles, etc.), one should be seated on a *darbhāsana* (a seat made of *kusa* grass) and performing his mental protection (by worshipping the deities of all directions), repeat the mantra (*Oṅkāra* i.e. OM) of *ratha maṇḍala*. -18.

Method of Oṅkāra Sādhanā

पद्मकं स्वस्तिकं वापि भद्रासनमथापि वा ।

बद्ध्वा योगासनं सम्यगुत्तराभिमुखः स्थितः ॥१९॥

padmakaṃ svastikaṃ vāpi bhadrāsanamathāpi vā /

badhvā yogāsanaṃ saṃyaguttarābhimukhaḥ sthitaḥ //19//

Having performed either *padma* or *svastika*, or *bhadra* āsana or any other comfortable pose, one should be seated in the *yogāsana* firmly and properly facing the north. -19.

नासिकापुटमङ्गुल्या पिधायैकेन मारुतम् ।

आकृष्य धारयेदग्निं शब्दमेव विचिन्तयेत् ॥२०॥

nāsikāpuṭamaṅgulyā pidhāyaikena mārutam /

ākṛṣya dhārayedagniṃ śabdameva vicintayet //20//

Then having closed the (right) nostril with the thumb, one should inhale through the opposite (left) nostril and retain *māruta* (the *vāyu*) inside (closing both nostrils). At that time he should contemplate on the word (sound OM) alone in the form of radiant fire. -20.

OM Is Brahma

ओमित्येकाक्षरं ब्रह्म ओमित्येतन्न रेचयेत् ।

दिव्यमन्त्रेण बहुधा कुर्यात्मलमुक्तये ॥२१॥

omityekāśaraṃ brahma omityetanna rechayet /

divyamantreṇa bahudhā kuryātmalamuktaye //21//

The monosyllable word OM is verily *Brahma*. So, one should perform *recaka* (or exhale the *vāyu* slowly) contemplating on OM alone. In this way, one should get rid of the mental impurities by the repetition of this divine mantra OM many times (along with the *prāṇāyāma* practice). -21.

Contemplation on OM

पश्चाद्ध्यायीत पूर्वोक्तक्रमशो मन्त्रविद्बुधः ।

स्थूलादिस्थूलसूक्ष्मं च नाभेरूर्ध्वमुपक्रमः ॥२२॥

paścāddhyāyīta pūrvoktakramaśo mantravidbudhaḥ /

sthūlādisthūlaśūkṣmaṃ ca nāverūrdhvamupakramaḥ //22//

Then the wise *mantravida* (who knows the practice, application and power a mantra) should contemplate on OM and perform *prāṇāyāma* according to aforesaid order. This type of *prāṇāyāma* should be performed above the navel region or in the area of heart, contemplating on (the Omnipresent Form, etc.) first at the gross and subtle and then at the subtlest levels. -22.

Method of Steady Practice

तिर्यगूर्ध्वमधोदृष्टिं विहाय च महामतिः ।

स्थिरस्थायी विनिष्कम्पः सदा योगं समभ्यसेत् ॥२३॥

tiryagūrdhvamadhodṛṣṭiṃ ca mahāmatiḥ /

sthirasthāyī viniṣkampaḥ sadā yogaṃ samabhyaset //23//

The man of high intellect should give up seeing crosswise, up or down and should always practice yoga properly in a steady manner without tremor. -23.

Practice of Dhāraṇā

तालमात्राविनिष्कम्पो धारणायोजनं तथा ।

द्वादशमात्रो योगस्तु कालतो नियमः स्मृतः ॥२४॥

tālamātrāviniṣkampo dhāraṇāyojanaṃ tathā /

dvādaśamātro yogastu kālato niyamaḥ smṛta //24//

The combination of *tāla* (rhythm) and *mātrā* (time measure or duration of time) in the practice of *dhāraṇā* should be carried out in a steady way. It is stated that this is the yoga of twelve *mātrās* as prescribed time duration. -24.

Nature of Praṇava

अघोषमव्यञ्जनमस्वरं च अतालुकण्ठोष्ठमनासिकं च यत् ।

अरेफजातमुभयोष्मवर्जितं यदक्षरं न क्षरते कथञ्चित् ॥२५॥

aghoṣamavyañjanamasvaraṃ atālu-

kaṇṭhoṣṭhaṃ anāsikaṃ ca yat /

arephajātamubhayoṣmavarjitaṃ yada-

kṣaraṃ na kṣarate kathañcit //25//

The word *praṇava* is *aghoṣa* (which is not pronounced by the external efforts). It is neither vowel nor consonant. It is neither palatal nor guttural nor labial nor nasal nor semi-vowel nor sibilant. It is *akṣara* (the sacred sound) which never perishes. -25.

Co-practice of Prāṇa and Mind

येनासौ गच्छते मार्गं प्राणस्तेन अभिगच्छति ।

अतस्तमभ्यसेन्नित्यं यन्मार्ग गमनाय वै ॥२६॥

yenāsau gacchate mārgaṃ prāṇastena abhigacchati /

atastamabhyasennityaṃ yanmārga gamanāya vai //26//

Wherever a yogi wants to go by the path of his mind, he travels through the same path with his *prāṇa* and mind together. Therefore, he should verily go on practicing regularly in order to follow the excellent path. -26.

Door Leading to Liberation

हृद्द्वारं वायुद्वारं च मूर्धद्वारं अथापरम् ।

मोक्षद्वारं बिलं चैव सुषिरं मण्डलं विदुः ॥२७॥

hṛddvāraṃ vāyudvāraṃ ca mūrdhadvāraṃ athāparam /

mokṣadvāraṃ bilaṃ caiva suṣiraṃ maṇḍalaṃ viduḥ //27//

The entering path of *vāyu* is the door of *hṛdaya* (heart). Above it and all, there is *mūrdhadvāra* (*brahmarandhra*). This is also called *mokṣadvāra* (the door leading to liberation) or *suṣira maṇḍala* (the hole leading to sphere of the sun). -27.

Prescribed Rules for a Yogi

भयं क्रोधमथालस्यमतिस्वप्नं अतिजागरम् ।

अत्याहारमनाहरं नित्यं योगी विवर्जयेत् ॥२८॥

bhayaṃ krodhamathālasyamatisvapnaṃ atijāgaram /

atyāhāramanāhāraṃ nityaṃ yogī vivarjayet //28//

A yogi should always give up fear, anger, indolence, too much sleeping, too much waking, too much eating and not eating at all. -28.

Arising of Wisdom

अनेन विधिना सम्यङ् नित्यमभ्यसते क्रमात् ।

स्वयमुत्पद्यते ज्ञानं त्रिभिर्मासैर्न संशयः ॥२९॥

anena vidhinā samyaṅ nityamabhyasyate kramāt /

svayamutpadyate jñānaṃ tribhirmāsairna saṃśayaḥ //29//

In this way, a *sādhaka* who practices regularly and gradually, spontaneous wisdom will arise itself in him within three months. There is no doubt about it.

Attainment of Kaivalya

चतुर्भिः पश्यते देवान्पञ्चभिर्विततः क्रमः ।

इच्छयाप्नोति कैवल्यं षष्ठे मासि न संशयः ॥३०॥

caturbhiḥ paśyate devānpañcabhirvitataḥ kramaḥ /

icchayāpnoti kaivalyaṃ ṣaṣṭhe māsi na saṃśayaḥ //30//

He will gain the ability to see *devatās* in four months. Gradually, he will achieve the power equal to gods in five months. He will verily achieve the power to attain *kaivalya* (liberation) at his will in six months. There is no doubt about it. -30.

Dhāraṇā on Praṇava Mātrās

पार्थिवः पञ्चमात्रस्तु चतुर्मात्रिस्तु वारुणः ।
आग्नेयस्तु त्रिमात्रोऽसौ वायव्यस्तु द्विमात्रकः ॥३१॥

pārthivaḥ pañcamātrastu caturmātrastu vāruṇaḥ /
āgneyastu trimātro'sau vāyavyastu dvimātrakaḥ //31//

One should meditate on *praṇava* of five *mātras* during the practice of *dhāraṇā* on the earth element, of four *mātras* during the practice of *dhāraṇā* on the water element, of three *mātras* during the practice of *dhāraṇā* on the fire element, of two *mātras* during the practice of *dhāraṇā* on the air element. -31.

एकमात्रस्तथाकाशो ह्यर्धमात्रं तु चिन्तयेत् ।
सिद्धिं कृत्वा तु मनसा चिन्तयेदात्मनात्मनि ॥३२॥

ekamātrastathākāśo hyardhamātraṃ tu cintayet /
sandhiṃ kṛtvā tu manasā cintayedātmanātmani //32//

Similarly, one should meditate on *praṇava* of one *mātra* during the practice of *dhāraṇā* on the ether element and contemplate on the half *mātra* of *praṇava* during its meditation. Having established connection by the mind, one should meditate on *Ātman* (having the form of *Oṅkāra* or OM) by his *Ātmā* (pure intelligence). -32.

Place of Prāṇa Vāyu

त्रिंशत्सार्धाङ्गुलः प्राणो यत्र प्राणैः प्रतिष्ठितः ।
एष प्राण इति ख्यातो बाह्यप्राणस्य गोचरः ॥३३॥

trimśatsārdhāṅgulaḥ prāṇo yatra prāṇaiḥ pratiṣṭhitaḥ /
eṣa prāṇa iti khyāto bāhyaprāṇasya gocaraḥ //33//

Wherein the thirty-half digits long *prāṇa* is abiding in the form of breath, there is the place of *prāṇa vāyu* (the region of the heart). This is the reason that it is known as *prāṇa*. The external *prāṇa* is observed (by the senses). -33.

Diurnal Count of Breath

अशीतिश्च शतं चैव सहस्राणि त्रयोदश ।

लक्षश्चैको विनिश्वास अहोरात्रप्रमाणतः ॥३४॥

aśītiśca śataṃ caiva sahastrāṇi trayodaśa /

lakṣaścaiko viniśvāsa ahorātrapramāṇataḥ //34//

The count of the breaths of the external *prāṇa* is one lakh thirteen thousand one hundred eighty in a day and night (24 hours). -34.

It should be noted that according to classical text *Svara Yoga*, the total count of breaths is twenty-one thousand six hundred in a day and a night, fifteen breaths per minute.

Location of Five Prāṇas

प्राण आद्यो हृदि स्थाने अपानस्तु पुनर्गुदे ।

समानो नाभिदेशे तु उदानः कण्ठमाश्रितः ॥३५॥

prāṇa ādhyo hṛdi sthāne apānastu punargude /

samāno nābhideśe tu udānaḥ kaṇṭhamāśritaḥ //35//

Ādhya (the first) *prāṇa* is located in the region of heart, *apāna* is located at the anus, *samāna* is located in the region of the navel and *udāna* is located in the region of the throat. -35.

व्यानः सर्वेषु चाङ्गेषु व्याप्य तिष्ठति सर्वदा ।

अथ वर्णास्तु पञ्चानां प्राणादीनामनुक्रमात् ॥३६॥

vyānaḥ sarveṣu cāṅgeṣu vyāpya tiṣṭhati sarvadā /

atha varṇāstu pañcānāṃ prāṇādīnāmanukramāt //36//

Vyāna always abides pervading all parts of the body. Now the colors of the five *prāṇa vāyus* are described according to their order. -36.

Colors of Five Prāṇas Vāyus

रक्तवर्णो मणिप्रख्यः प्राणवायुः प्रकीर्तितः ।

अपानस्तस्य मध्ये तु इन्द्रगोपसमप्रभः ॥३७॥

raktavarṇo maṇiprakhyaḥ prāṇavāyuḥ prakīrtitaḥ /

apānastasya madhye tu indragopasamaprabhaḥ //37//

It is said that the color of the *prāṇa vāyu* is of like red shining pearl (gem). The color of the *apāna vāyu* in the middle of the anus is deep red shining like *indragopa* (the cochineal insect). -37.

समानस्तु द्वयोर्मध्ये गोक्षीरधवलप्रभः ।

आपाण्डुर उदानश्च व्यानो ह्यर्चिःसमप्रभः ॥३८॥

samānastu dvayormadhye gokṣīradhavalaprabhaḥ /

āpāṇḍura udānaśca vyāno hyarciḥsamaprabhaḥ //38//

Samāna in the middle of the former two (in the navel region between *prāṇa* and *apāna*) is of the color of cow's milk or bright white. *Udāna* is of the color of whitish yellow. *Vyāna* is of the color of bright flame (of fire). -38.

No Rebirth After Penetration of Maṇḍala

यस्येदं मण्डलं भित्वा मारुतो याति मूर्धनि ।

यत्र कुत्र म्रियेद्वापि न स भूयोऽबिजायते ।

न स भूयोऽभिजायत इत्युपनिषत् ॥३९॥

yasyedaṃ maṇḍalaṃ bhitvā māruto yāti mūrdhani /

yatra kutra mṛyedvāpi na sa bhūyo'bhijāyate

na sa bhūyo'bhijāyata ityupaniśat //39//

The great yogi whose *prāṇa* penetrates this *maṇḍala* (the region of five elements and five *prāṇas*) and reaches the region of the head (*sahasrāra*), wherever he may depart his life, he will not be born again, he will not be born again. Thus (ends) the *upaniśat*. -39.

शान्तिपाठः

ॐ सह नाववतु । सह नौ भुनक्तु । सह वीर्यं करवावहै ।

तेजस्विनावधीतमस्तु मा विद्विषावहै ॥

ॐ शान्तिः शान्तिः शान्तिः ॥

Śāntipāṭhaḥ

oṃ saha nāvavatu / saha nau bhunaktu /

saha vīryaṃ karavāvahai /

tejasvināvadhītamastu mā vidviṣāvahai /

oṃ śāntiḥ śāntiḥ śāntiḥ //

OM. May He protect both of us together. May He nourish both of us together. May both of us get strength and power together. May our knowledge (given and received between us) be powerful. May there be no animosity between us. Om. May there be peace, peace and peace again in all the three worlds. May the three types of pains/miseries be peaceful.

इति कृष्णयजुर्वेदीय अमृतनादोपनिषत्समाप्ता ॥

Thus here ends the *Amṛtanāda Upaniṣad* belonging to

Krishna Yajurveda

AMṚTABINDU UPANIṢAD

अमृतबिन्दु उपनिषद्

Book Two

English Translation Accompanied by Sanskrit Text in Roman Transliteration

Translated into English by
Swami Vishnuswaroop

Divine Yoga Institute
Kathmandu, Nepal

INTRODUCTION

Of twenty *Yoga Upaniṣads, Amṛtabindu* is an important *Upaniṣad* belonging to *Krisṇa Yajurveda. Amṛta bindu* literally means a drop of immortal nectar. It contains twenty-two mantras as drops of spiritual teaching which lead to immortality. Even though it is considered as a minor *Upaniṣad,* the significance of its spiritual teaching is great and important like other *Upaniṣads.*

This *Upaniṣad* mainly discusses on the nature of the mind, cause of bondage and liberation, duty of spiritual seekers, achievement of *parama pada,* real *jñāna* and *dhyāna,* nature of the *Brahman, saguṇa* and *nirguṇa dhyāna,* qualities of the *Brahman,* nature of the supreme state, existence *Bhūtātmā* in all, changeless nature of *Ātman, Om* as *Parabrahman,* renunciation for the attainment of ultimate wisdom, meditation on the *Parabrahman,* etc. and finally, realization of "I am That *Brahman* or *Vāsudeva*" Who is complete, immobile and tranquil, the abode and indweller of all.

Publisher

ŚĀNTIPĀṬHAḤ

शान्तिपाठ:

ॐ सह नाववतु । सह नौ भुनक्तु । सह वीर्यं करवावहै ।

तेजस्विनावधीतमस्तु मा विद्विषावहै ॥

ॐ शान्तिः शान्तिः शान्तिः ॥

oṃ saha nāvavatu / saha nau bhunaktu /

saha vīryaṃ karavāvahai /

tejasvināvadhītamastu mā vidviṣāvahai /

oṃ śāntiḥ śāntiḥ śāntiḥ //

OM. May He protect both of us together. May He nourish both of us together. May both of us get strength and power together. May our knowledge (given and received between us) be powerful. May there be no animosity between us. Om. May there be peace, peace and peace again in all the three worlds. May the three types of pains/miseries be peaceful.

BOOK TWO

Amṛtabindu Upaniṣad

अमृतबिन्दु उपनिषद्

Two Kinds of Mind

मनो हि द्विविधं प्रोक्तं शुद्धं चाशुद्धमेव च ।

अशुद्धं कामसंकल्पं शुद्धं कामविवर्जितम् ॥१॥

mano hi dvividhaṃ proktaṃ śuddhaṃ cāśuddhameva ca /

aśuddhaṃ kāmasaṅkalpaṃ śuddhaṃ kāmavivarjitam //1//

It is said that the mind is of two kinds – *śuddha* (pure) and *aśuddha* (impure). The impure mind has craving and desire, and the pure mind has no craving. -1.

Cause of Bondage and Liberation

मन एव मनुष्याणां कारणं बन्धमोक्षयोः ।

बन्धाय विषयासक्तं मुक्त्यै निर्विषयं स्मृतम् ॥२॥

mana eva manuṣyāṇāṃ kāraṇaṃ bandhamokṣayoḥ /

bandhāya viṣayāsaktaṃ muktaye nirviṣayaṃ smṛtam //2//

The mind of men is surely the cause of bondage and liberation. It is thought that the mind attached to sense and their objects falls in bondage and the mind free from desire and craving is liberated. -2.

Duty of Spiritual Seekers

यतो निर्विषयस्यास्य मनसो मुक्तिरिष्यते ।

अतो निर्विषयं नित्यं मनः कार्यं मुमुक्षुणा ॥३॥

yato nirviṣyasyāsya manaso muktiriṣyate /

ato nirviṣayaṃ nityaṃ manaḥ kāryaṃ mumukṣuṇā //3//

As the mind free from desire is sought for (attaining) liberation, so, it is the duty of spiritual seekers of liberation that the mind is constantly made free from desires.

Achievement of Parama Pada

निरस्तविषयासङ्गं संनिरुद्धं मनो हृदि ।

यदाऽऽयात्यात्मनो भावं तदा तत्परमं पदम् ॥४॥

nirastaniṣayāsaṅgaṃ sanniruddhaṃ mano hṛdi /

yadā''yātyātmano bhāvaṃ tadā tatparaṃ padam //4//

When the mind is thrown out of the association of the desire, entirely controlled in the heart and established in its true nature there, then *parama pada* (the Supreme State) is attained. -4.

Real Jñāna and Dhyāna

तावदेव निरोद्धव्यं यावधृति गतं क्षयम् ।

एतज्ज्ञानं च ध्यानं च शेषो न्यायश्च विस्तरः ॥५॥

tāvadeva niroddhavyaṃ yāvaddhṛti gataṃ kṣayam /

etajñānaṃ ca dhyānaṃ ca śeṣo nyāyaśca vistaraḥ //5//

The mind should be controlled until it is destroyed there (in the heart). This is *jñāna* (wisdom) and as well as *dhyāna* (meditation) and the rest is simply an extension of logical argument. -5.

Nature of the Brahman

नैव चिन्त्यं न चाचिन्त्यं न चिन्त्यं चिन्त्यमेव च ।

पक्षपातविनिर्मुक्तं ब्रह्म सम्पद्यते तदा ॥६॥

naiva cintyaṃ na cacintyaṃ na cintyaṃ cintyameva ca /

pakṣapātavinirmuktaṃ brahma sampadhyate tadā //6//

It is neither to be thought of nor not to be thought of nor certainly to be thought of for the sake of thinking over it (that state). When it is free from all types of partiality, then the *Brahman* is attained. -6.

Saguṇa and Nirguṇa Dhyāna with OM

स्वरेण संधयेद्योगमस्वरं भावयेत्परम् ।

अस्वरेणानुभावेन नाभावो भाव इष्यते ॥७॥

svareṇa sandhayeddhyogamasvaraṃ bhāvayetparam /

asvareṇānubhāvena nābhāvo bhāva iṣyate //7//

One should (first of all) combine the yoga of monosyllable OM (with its *mātrās*) to contemplate on the Supreme (in its *Saguṇa* form) and then meditate on the Supreme (in its *Nirguṇa* form) beyond all (*mātrās* of OM). By the realization of *asvara* (existence beyond all), one recognizes the omnipresence of the Supreme (and non-existence of the mundane world). -7.

Qualities of the Brahman

तदेव निष्कलं ब्रह्म निर्विकल्पं निरञ्जनम् ।

तद्ब्रह्माहमिति ज्ञात्वा ब्रह्म सम्पद्यते ध्रुवम् ॥८॥

tadeva niṣkalaṃ brahma nirvikalpaṃ nirañjanam /

tadabrahmāhamiti jñātvā brahma sampadhyate dhruvam //8//

That alone is *Brahma* who is without any parts or limbs, without any (or beyond all) distinction and without any fault. Having known that "I am that *Brahman*", one verily attains the *Brahman*. –8.

निर्विकल्पमनन्तं च हेतुदृष्टान्तवर्जितम् ।

अप्रमेयमनादिं च यज्ज्ञात्वा मुच्यते बुधः ॥९॥

nirvikalpamanantaṃ ca hetudyāṣṭāntavarjitam /

aprameyamanādiṃ ca yajjñātvā mucyate budhaḥ //9//

He is indeterminate, infinite, beyond reason and example, without cause, and beyond all proofs and without beginning. By knowing it, the wise becomes free. -9.

Nature of the Supreme State

न निरोधो न चोत्पत्तिर्न बद्धो न च साधकः ।

न मुमुक्षुर्न वै मुक्त इत्येषा परमार्थता ॥१०॥

na norodho na cotpattirna baddho na ca sādhakaḥ /

na mumukṣurna vai mukta ityeṣā paramarthatā //10//

Neither there is dissolution nor creation, neither one is bound nor one is spiritual aspirant, neither one is the seeker after freedom nor one is liberated. This is the supreme state. -10.

No Birth Beyond Three States

एक एवात्मा मन्तव्यो जाग्रत्स्वप्नसुषुप्तिषु ।

स्थानत्रयव्यतीतस्य पुनर्जन्म न विद्यते ॥११॥

eka evātmā mantavyo jāgratsvapnasuṣuptiṣu /

sthānatrayavyatītasya punarjanma na vidyate //11//

Certainly, the *Ātmān* should be considered as one alone throughout the waking, dreaming and sleeping states. There is no rebirth for him who has transcended these three states. -11.

Bhūtātmā Exists in All

एक एव हि भूतात्मा भूते भूते व्यवस्थितः ।

एकधा बहुधा चैव दृश्यते जलचन्द्रवत् ॥१२॥

eka eva hi bhūtātmā bhūte bhūte vyavasthita /

ekadhā bahudhā caiva dṛṣyate jalacandravat //12//

The *Bhūtātmā* (the Soul of all beings) is one alone and is situated in all beings. He is only one, but seen as many just like the reflection of the moon in the water (of the various vessels). -12.

Ātman is Changeless

घटसम्वृतमाकाशं नीयमानो घटे यथा ।

घटो नीयेत नाऽकाशः तद्वज्जीवो नभोपमः ॥१३॥

ghaṭasaṃvṛtamākāśaṃ nīyamāno ghaṭe yathā /

ghaṭo nīyeta nā'kāśaḥ tatdhājjīvo nabhopamaḥ //13//

Just like a pot carried from one place to another changes its places and not the *ākāśa* (ether) inside the pot. So also is the *Jīva* (*Ātmā*) which resembles the *ākāśa* (ether). -13.

घटवद्विविधाकारं भिद्यमानं पुनः पुनः ।

तद्भेदे न च जानाति स जानाति च नित्यशः ॥१४॥

ghaṭavadvividhākāraṃ bhidyamānaṃ punaḥ punaḥ /

tadbhede na ca jānāti sa jānāti ca nityaśaḥ //14//

Just like the pot takes various forms and is fit to be varied again and again so is if one (can differentiate and) knows that (the destruction of pot is not the destruction of the ether), then he knows the Eternal. -14.

Illusion Leads Nowhere

शब्दमायावृतो नैव तमसा याति पुष्करे ।

भिन्नो तमसि चैकत्वमेक एवानुपश्यति ॥१५॥

śabdamāyāvṛto naiva tamasā yāti puṣkare /

bhinno tamasi caikatvameka evānupaśyati //15//

One who is encircled by the illusion of *śabda* (name and its form) cannot reach the pilgrimage (holy place of *Ātmān*) just like one (cannot reach anywhere) in darkness. When darkness (illusion) is removed, then he sees the oneness of the One (*Ātmān*) alone. -15.

OM in the Form Parabrahma

शब्दाक्षरं परं ब्रह्म तस्मिन्क्षीणे यदक्षरम् ।

तद्विद्वानक्षरं ध्यायेद्यदीच्छेच्छान्तिमात्मनः ॥१६॥

śabdākṣaraṃ paraṃ brahma tasmiṇśīṇe yadakṣaram /

tadvidvānakṣaraṃ dhyāyecdyadīcchechāntimātmanaḥ //16//

The *śabdākṣara* (monosyllable word OM) is to be understood as *Parama Brahma* (the Supreme *Brahman*). When it is destroyed (the ideation of the OM as word), then there exists the *Akṣara* (Imperishable One). The wise one should contemplate on that (Imperishable One or *Brahman*) if he desires for the peace of his *Ātman*. -16.

Two Types of Vidyās

द्वे विद्ये वेदितव्ये तु शब्दब्रह्म परं च यत् ।

शब्दब्रह्मणि निष्णातः परं ब्रह्माधिगच्छति ॥१७॥

dve vidye veditavye tu śabdabrahma paraṃ ca yat /

śabdabrahmāṇi nidkṇātaḥ paraṃ brahmādhigacchati //17//

The two types of *vidyās* (branches of special wisdom or knowledge) to be studied are *Śabdabrahma* and the *Brahman* beyond it. One who is expert in *Śabdabrahma* reaches the Supreme *Brahman*. -17.

Renunciation for Gaining Wisdom

ग्रन्थमभ्यस्य मेधावी ज्ञानविज्ञानतत्परः ।

पलालमिव धान्यार्थी त्यजेद्ग्रन्थमशेषतः ॥१८॥

granthamabhysya medhāvī jñānavījñānatatparaḥ /

palālamiva dhānyārthi tyajedgranthamaśeṣataḥ //18//

Having studied the scriptures (on the knowledge of *Brahman*), the wise man who is committed to gain spiritual knowledge and wisdom, should abandon the books in totality just like the man who wants to get (uncooked) rice abandons the husks. -18.

Milk Is the Same From Multi-colored Cows

गवामनेकवर्णानां क्षीरस्याप्येकवर्णता ।

क्षीरवत्पश्यते ज्ञानं लिङ्गिनस्तु गवां यथा ॥१९॥

gavāmanekavarṇānāṃ kṣīrasyāpyekavarṇatā /

kṣīravatpaṣyate jñānaṃ liṅginastu gavāṃ yathā //19//

The white color of the milk is the same of all cows having various colors. The wise man regards the knowledge as milk and the various branches of knowledge (of the *Brahman*) as the cows. -19.

Churning the Mind for Ultimate Knowledge

घृतमिव पयसि निगूढं भूते भूते च वसति विज्ञानम् ।

सततं मनसि मन्थयितव्यं मनो मन्थानभूतेन ॥२०॥

ghṛtamiva payasi nigūḍhaṃ bhūte bhūte ca vasati vijñānam /

satataṃ manasi manthayitavyaṃ mano manthānabhūtena //20//

Just like the butter is hidden in milk, similarly, the *vijñāna* (knowledge of the *Brahman*) remains hiding in all beings. So, one should constantly churn his mind (for this knowledge) by the churning stick of the mind. -20.

Meditation on the Parabrahman

ज्ञाननेत्रं समाधाय चोद्धरेद्वह्निवत्परम् ।
निष्कलं निश्चलं शान्तं तद्ब्रह्माहमिति स्मृतम् ॥२१॥

jñānanetraṃ samādhāya coddharedvanhigavatparam /
niṣkalaṃ niścalaṃ śāntaṃ tadbrahmāhamiti smṛtam //21//

Just like the sacrificial fire is obtained (by churning the wood) one should acquire the *Param* (Ultimate *Brahman*) by meditating properly (on Him) with the eye of the knowledge. Thus, he should recollect that "I am that *Brahman*" Who is complete, immobile and tranquil. -2.

Vāsudeva Abode of All and Dwells in All

सर्वभूताधिवासं यद्भूतेषु च वसत्यपि ।
सर्वानुग्राहकत्वेन तदस्म्यहं वासुदेवः ॥२२॥

sarvabhūtādhivāsaṃ yadbhuteṣu ca vasatyapi /
sarvānugrāhakatvena tadsmyahaṃ vāsudevaḥ //22//

Even though He is the abode of all beings, He also dwells in all beings due to his grace to one and all. I am that *Vāsudeva* (Lord of the Universe). -22.

शान्तिपाठः

ॐ सह नाववतु । सह नौ भुनक्तु । सह वीर्यं करवावहै ।
तेजस्विनावधीतमस्तु मा विद्विषावहै ॥
ॐ शान्तिः शान्तिः शान्तिः ॥

Śānti Pāṭha

oṃ saha nāvavatu /
saha nau bhunaktu /
saha vīryaṃ karavāvahai /
tejasvināvadhītamastu mā vidviṣāvahai /
oṃ śāntiḥ śāntiḥ śāntiḥ //

Om. May He protect both of us together. May He nourish both of us together. May both of us get strength and power together. May our knowledge (given and received between us) be powerful. May there be no animosity between us. Om. May there be peace, peace and peace again in all the three worlds. May the three types of pains/miseries be peaceful.

इति कृष्ण यजुर्वेदेऽमृतबिन्दूपनिषद् समाप्ता ॥

Thus ends the *Amṛtabindu Upaniṣad* belonging to

Krishna Yajurveda.

KṢURIKĀ UPANIṢAD

क्षुरिका उपनिषद्

Book Three

English Translation Accompanied by Sanskrit

Text in Roman Transliteration

Translated into English by

Swami Vishnuswaroop

Divine Yoga Institute

Kathmandu, Nepal

INTRODUCTION

Kṣurikā Upaniṣad belongs to *Kriṣna Yajurveda.* There are twenty-five mantras in this *Upaniṣad.* This *Upaniṣad* is like a sharp knife to cut off the barriers on the path of the realization of the ultimate truth. Of the eight limbs of the yoga, it mainly discusses on the perfection of *dhāraṇā* and its results.

According to this *Upaniṣad,* first of all one should be seated in a stable āsana and circulate the *prāṇa* through the *prāṇic* pathways on all the vital parts of the body by performing the practice of *prāṇāyāma* just like a spider that keeps moving on the spider-net created by it. Then he should gradually move upward circulating the *prāṇa* from the perineum to the heart, penetrate the seventy-two thousand *nāḍīs* and then finally reach the spot of *Parabrahma* where he is able to cut off the bondage of all the karmas and dissolves himself into the *Paramātman* just like the flame of a lamp after burning all the oil and wicks disappears into its cause. This is the teaching of this *Upaniṣad.* Thus, the practice of *dhāraṇā,* one of the major components of yoga with its ultimate goal is presented in this *Upaniṣad.*

Publisher

ŚĀNTIPĀṬHAḤ

शान्तिपाठः

ॐ सह नाववतु । सह नौ भुनक्तु । सह वीर्यं करवावहै ।

तेजस्विनावधीतमस्तु मा विद्विषावहै ॥

ॐ शान्तिः शान्तिः शान्तिः ॥

oṃ saha nāvavatu /
saha nau bhunaktu /
saha vīryaṃ karavāvahai /
tejasvināvadhītamastu mā vidviṣāvahai /
oṃ śāntiḥ śāntiḥ śāntiḥ //

OM. May He protect both of us together. May He nourish both of us together. May both of us get strength and power together. May our knowledge (given and received between us) be powerful. May there be no animosity between us. Om. May there be peace, peace and peace again in all the three worlds. May the three types of pains/miseries be peaceful.

BOOK THREE

Kṣurikā Upaniṣad

क्षुरिका उपनिषद्

Discourse on Dhāraṇā

क्षुरिकां सम्प्रवक्ष्यामि धारणां योगसिद्धये ।
यां प्राप्य न पुनर्जन्म योगयुक्तस्य जायते ॥१॥
वेदतत्त्वार्थविहितं यथोक्तं हि स्वयंभुवा ।

kṣurikāṃ sampravakṣyāmi dhāraṇāṃ yogasiddhaye /
yāṃ prāpya na punarjanma yogayuktasya jāyate //1//
vedatattvārthavihitaṃ yathoktaṃ hi svayaṃbhuvā /

I am giving an account of *dhāraṇā* (concentration) like a *kṣurikā* (sharp knife) in order to attain perfection in yoga. After getting it, one who establishes him in this yoga, there will be no rebirth for him. It contains the essence of *Veda* as said by *Svayaṃbhu* (the *Brahmā*). - 1.

Practice of Prāṇāyāma with Praṇava

निःशब्दं देशमास्थाय तत्रासनमवस्थितः ॥२॥
कूर्मोऽङ्गानीव संहृत्य मनो हृदि निरुध्य च ।
मात्राद्वादशयोगेन प्रणवेन शनैः शनैः ॥३॥
पूरयेत्सर्वमात्मानं सर्वद्वारं निरुध्य च ।
उरोमुखकटिग्रीवं किञ्चिद्धृयमुन्नतम् ॥४॥
प्राणान्सन्धारयेत्तस्मिनासाभ्यन्तरचारिणः ।
भूत्वा तत्र गतप्राणः शनैरथ समुत्सृजेत् ॥५॥

niḥśabdaṃ deśamāsthāya tatrāsanamavasthitaḥ //2//

kūrmoṅgānīva saṃhṛtya mano hṛdi nirudhya ca /

mātrādvādaśayogena praṇavena śanaiḥ śanaiḥ //3//

pūrayetsarvamātmānaṃ sarvadvāraṃ nirudhya ca /

uromukhakaṭigrīvaṃ kiñciddhṛdayamunnatam //4//

prāṇānsandhārayettasminnāsābhyantaracariṇaḥ /

bhūtvā tatra gataprāṇaḥ śanairatha samutsṛjet //5//

One should sit in a comfortable pose in a place where there are not any noises/sounds. Then he should withdraw his mind like a tortoise (withdraws its limbs) and restrain it in his heart and slowly he should inhale *prāṇa* by using the same length and duration of twelve *mātrās* of *praṇava* and fill up the entire *Ātman* (body). One should close all the doors of *prāṇa* during this period (practice) and (at the same time) should slightly raise his chest, mouth, waist, neck and heart. He should hold the *prāṇa* inhaled through the nostrils in all parts of the body. Once the *prāṇa* has reached everywhere in the body, then he should exhale it slowly. -2-5.

Circulation of Prāṇa on Vital Parts

स्थिरमात्राद्दृढं कृत्वा अङ्गुष्ठेन समाहितः ।

द्वे गुल्फे तु प्रकुर्वीत जङ्घे चैव त्रयस्त्रयः ॥६॥

द्वे जानुनी तथोरुभ्यां गुदे शिश्ने त्रयस्त्रयः ।

वायोरायतनं चात्र नाभिदेशे समाश्रयेत् ॥७॥

sthiramātrādṛḍhaṃ kṛtvā aṅguṣṭhena samāhitaḥ /

dve gulphe tu prakurvīta jaṅghe caiva trayastrayaḥ //6//

dve jānunī tathorubhyāṃ gude śiśne trayastrayaḥ /

vāyorāyatanaṃ cātra nābhideśe samāśrayet //7//

When the *prāṇāyāma* (with *Dhāraṇā*) becomes stable, one should attentively concentrate on the circulation of *prāṇa* twice on the two ankles along with the toes, thrice on the (areas between ankles and knees) shanks and thighs, twice on the knees and thighs and thrice on the anus and the genital area. Then he should concentrate the *prāṇa* on the navel region. -6-7.

Nāḍīs and Their Color

तत्र नाडी सुषुम्ना तु नाडीभिर्बहुभिर्वृता ॥

अणुरक्ताश्च पीताश्च कृष्णास्ताम्रविलोहिताः ॥८॥

tatra nāḍī suṣumnā tu nāḍībhirbahubhirvṛtā /

aṇuraktāśca pītāśca kṛṣṇāstāmravilohitāḥ //8//

There is the *suṣumnā nāḍī* surrounded by ten *nāḍīs*. Those various subtle *nāḍīs* are of red, yellow, black and copper color. -8.

अतिसूक्ष्मां च तन्वीं च शुक्लां नाडीं समाश्रयेत् ।

तत्र संचारयेत्प्राणानूर्णनाभीव तन्तुना ॥९॥

atisūkṣmāṃ ca tanvīṃ ca śuklāṃ nāḍīṃ samāśrayet /

tataḥ saṃcārayetprāṇānūrṇanābhīva tantunā //9//

There one should take shelter on the *nāḍī* which is very subtle, thin and white. A yogi should circulate his concentrated *prāṇa* on the sphere of that *nāḍī* just like a spider moves on the net created by its own saliva. -9.

The Regions of Dahara and Manas

ततो रक्तोत्पलाभासं हृदयातनं महत्

दहरं पुण्डरीकं तद् वेदान्तेषु निगद्यते ॥१०॥

तद्भित्त्वा कण्ठमायाति तां नाडीं पूरयन्यतः ।

मनसस्तु परं गृह्य सुतीक्ष्णं बुद्धिनिर्मलम् ॥११॥

tato raktotpalābhāsaṃ hṛdayātanaṃ mahat /

daharaṃ puṇḍarīkaṃ tadvedānteṣu nigadyate //10//

tadbhittvā kaṇṭhamāyāti tāṃ nāḍīṃ pūrayanyataḥ /

manasastu paraṃ guhyaṃ sutīkṣṇaṃ buddhinirmalam //11//

There (after the navel region) is a great sanctuary of heart region which is always radiant like red-colored lotus. It is called *dahara* or *puṇḍarīka* in *vedānta*. The *prāṇa* reaches the throat (after penetrating the heart region) filling the *nāḍīs* by the current of the *prāṇa*. After it (the throat) there is the region of the *manas* and beyond it there is the region of secret, sharp and pure *buddhi* (the intellect). -10-11.

Penetration of the Vital Regions

पादस्योपरि यन्मर्म तद्रूपं नाम चिन्तयेत् ।
मनोद्वारेण तीक्ष्णेन योगमाश्रित्य नित्यशः ॥१२॥
इन्द्रवज्र इति प्रोक्तं मर्मजङ्घानुकृन्तनम् ।
तद्ध्यानबलयोगेन धारणाभिर्निकृन्तयेत् ॥१३॥
ऊर्वोर्मध्ये तु संस्थाप्य मर्मप्राणविमोचनम् ।
चतुरभ्यासयोगेन छिन्देदनभिशङ्कितः ॥१४॥

pādasyopari yanmadhye tadrūpaṃ nāma cintayet /
manodvāreṇa tīkṣṇena yogamāśritya nityaśaḥ //12//
indravajra iti proktaṃ marmajaṅghānukṛntanam /
taddhyānabalayogena dhāraṇābhirnikṛntayet //13//
ūrvormadhye tu saṃsthāpya marmaprāṇavimocanam /
caturabhyāsayogena chindedanabhiśaṅkitaḥ //14//

In this way, one should contemplate on the names and forms of the vital parts (of the body) above the feet. He should penetrate the area named *indravajra* (the bolt of *Indra*) located in the thighs with a sharp razor of the mind by constantly taking refuge in yoga (practice). There by establishing the *prāṇa* freeing the vital regions between the thighs with the strength of the yoga of meditation and being free from all doubts he should penetrate all four vital regions (from the perineum to the heart) by the sharp concentration of the mind through the practice of yoga. -12-14.

Suṣumnā and Other Nāḍīs

ततः कण्ठान्तरे योगी समूहं नाडिसञ्चयम् ।
एकोत्तरं नाडिशतं तासां मध्ये पराः स्थिराः ॥१५॥
सुषुम्ना तु परे लीना विरजा ब्रह्मरूपिणी ।
इडा तिष्ठति वामेन पिङ्गला दक्षिणेन च ॥१६॥

tataḥ kaṇṭhāntare yogī samūhaṃ nāḍīsañcayam /

ekottaraṃ nāḍiśataṃ tāsāṃ madhye parā sthirā //15//

suṣumnā tu pare līnā virajā brahmarūpiṇī /

iḍā tiṣṭhati vāmena piṅgalā dakṣiṇena ca //16//

Then the yogi should circulate his *prāṇa* on the group of *nāḍīs* located in the throat. There are one hundred one *nāḍīs* in that group of *nāḍīs*. *Parā* (*śakti*) is located in the middle of them. *Suṣumnā nāḍī* remains absorbed into *Parama* (the Ultimate *Brahman*). *Virajā nāḍī* is identical with or in the form of the *Brahman*. *Iḍā* is located on the left side and *piṅgalā* is located on the right side. -15-16.

The Real Knower of the Truth

तयोर्मध्ये वरं स्थानं यस्तं वेद स वेदवित् ।

द्वासप्ततिसहस्राणि प्रति नाडीषु तैतिलम् ॥१७॥

tayormadhye varaṃ sthānaṃ yastaṃ veda sa vedavit /

dvāsaptatisahasrāṇi prati nāḍīṣu taitilam //17//

Between these two *nāḍīs* there is an excellent place. One who knows it, is the knower of the *Veda* (the ultimate truth). The total number of all subtle *nāḍīs* are said to be seventy-two thousands which are called *taitila*. -17.

Dhyāna Yoga Penetrates All Nāḍīs

छिद्यते ध्यानयोगेन सुषुम्नैका न छिद्यते ।

योगनिर्मलधारेण क्षुरेणानलवर्चसा ॥१८॥

छिन्देन्नाडीशतं धीरः प्रभावादिह जन्मनि ।

जातीपुष्पसमायोगैर्यथा वास्यति वै तिलम् ॥१९॥

chindyate dhyānayogena suṣumnaikā na chidyate /

yoganirmaladhāreṇa kṣureṇānalavarcasā //18//

chindennāḍīśataṃ dhīraḥ prabhāvādiha janmani /

jātīpuṣpasamāyogairyathā vāsyati vai tilam //19//

All the *nāḍīs* are penetrated by the yoga of *dhyāna* (contemplation), but *Suṣumnā* is only one *nāḍī* which can not be penetrated.

The self-possessed yogi due to the effect of the fire-like splendor of the pure sharpness of yoga and with the *dhāraṇā* identical to a sharp knife should penetrate thousand of *nāḍīs* in this life. All the *nāḍīs* become full of fragrance through this yoga just like the aroma of sesame (oil) is spread from a *jātī* (jasmine) flower. -18-19.

Freedom from Rebirth

एवं शुभाशुभैर्भावैः सा नाडी तां विभावयेत् ।

तद्भाविताः प्रपद्यन्ते पुनर्जन्मविवर्जिताः ॥२०॥

evaṃ śubhāśubhairbhāvaiḥ sā nāḍī tāṃ vibhāvayet /

tadbhāvitāḥ prapadyante punarjanmavivarjitāḥ //20//

In this way, all the *nāḍīs* should be considered having their good or bad nature or qualities. When the *dhāraṇā* is made stable on the *suṣumnā nāḍī,* a yogi becomes free from his rebirth. -20.

Victory Over the Mind By Tapa

तपोविजितचित्तस्तु निःशब्दं देशमास्थितः ।

निःसङ्गतत्त्वयोगज्ञो निरपेक्षः शनैः शनैः ॥२१॥

tapovijitacittastu niḥśabdaṃ deśamāsthitaḥ /

niḥsaṅgastattvayogajño nirapekṣaḥ śanaiḥ śanaiḥ //21//

One who has gained victory over his mind by *tapa* (austerity), remaining in an isolated place without any noises; he should be an adept of the essence of the yoga of detachment and gradually should attain a desireless state. -21.

Freedom from Bondage

पाशं छित्त्वा यथा हम्सो निर्विशङ्कः खमुत्क्रमेत् ।

छिन्नपाशस्तथा जीवः संसारं तरते सदा ॥२२॥

pāśaṃ chittvā yathā haṃso nirviśaṅkaḥ khamutkramet /

chinnapāśastathā jīvaḥ saṃsāraṃ tarate sadā //22//

Just like a swan after cutting the net of bondage being free from any doubts flies up in the sky, similarly a yogi after breaking all bondage (through the practice of this yoga) becomes free (from the bondage) and crosses the ocean of the world forever. -22.

Attainment of Laya

यथा निर्वाणकाले तु दीपो दग्ध्वा लयं व्रजेत् ।
तथा सर्वाणि कर्माणि योगी दग्ध्वा लयं व्रजेत् ॥२३॥

yathā nirvāṇakāle tu dīpo dagdhvā layaṃ vrajet /
tathā sarvāṇi karmāṇi yogi dagdhvā layaṃ vrajet //23//

Just the way during the time of extinction of the flame of a lamp having burnt all the oil and wicks dissolves itself (into its cause), similarly a yogi also having burnt down all the effects of his karmas in the fire of yoga dissolves himself (into the *Paramātman*). -23.

प्राणायामसुतीक्ष्णेन मात्राधारेण योगवित् ।
वैराग्योपलघृष्टेन छित्त्वा तं तु न बध्यते ॥२४॥

prāṇāyāmasutīkṣṇena mātrādhāreṇa yogavit /
vairāgyopalaghṛṣṭena chitvā taṃ tu na badhyate //24//

The knower of yoga who cuts off the ropes of the worldly subjects by sharpening the *dhāraṇā* like a sharp knife combining the *mātrās* (of AUM) on the stone of detachment cannot be bound (by the worldly bondage). -24.

Attainment of Immortal State

अमृतत्वं समाप्नोति यदा कामात्प्रमुच्यते ।
सर्वैषणाविनिर्मुक्तश्छित्त्वा तन्तुं न बध्यते
छित्त्वा तन्तुं न बध्यते । इत्युपनिषत् ॥

amṛtatvaṃ samāpnoti yadā kāmātpramucyate /
sarvaiṣaṇāvinirmuktaśchittvā tantuṃ
na badhyate chittvā tatuṃ na badhyate /
ityupaniṣat //25//

When the yogi is detached from desires and becomes free from all type of cravings and having cut off the ropes (of the bondage of all the worldly subjects), he can attain the immortal state and then he is not bound by the worldly bondage again. Having cut off the ropes, he is not bound by the worldly bondage again. Thus is the (teaching of) *Kṣurika Upaniṣat.* -25.

शान्तिपाठः

ॐ सह नाववतु । सह नौ भुनक्तु । सह वीर्यं करवावहै ।

तेजस्विनावधीतमस्तु मा विद्विषावहै ॥

ॐ शान्तिः शान्तिः शान्तिः ॥

Śānti Pāṭhaḥ

oṃ saha nāvavatu /

saha nau bhunaktu /

saha vīryaṃ karavāvahai /

tejasvināvadhītamastu mā vidviṣāvahai /

oṃ śāntiḥ śāntiḥ śānt/

OM. May He protect both of us together. May He nourish both of us together. May both of us get strength and power together. May our knowledge (given and received between us) be powerful. May there be no animosity between us. Om. May there be peace, peace and peace again in all the three worlds. May the three types of pains/miseries be peaceful.

॥ इति क्षुरिकोपनिषत्समाप्ता ॥

Thus ends the *Kṣurikā Upaniṣad.*

YOGARĀJA UPANIṢAD

योगराज उपनिषद्

Book Three

English Translation Accompanied by Sanskrit

Text in Roman Transliteration

Translated into English by

Swami Vishnuswaroop

Divine Yoga Institute

Kathmandu, Nepal

INTRODUCTION

This *Upaniṣad* belongs to yoga. Of the twenty *Yoga Upaniṣads*, it is an excellent yoga *Upanishad*. This is why this *Upaniṣad* is called *Yogarāja*. The theoretical aspect of yoga is described in detail in a simplified way in twenty-one verses. First of all, the four yogas - *Mantrayoga, Layayoga, Rājayoga* and *Haṭhayoga* are mentioned. Then the four limbs of yoga - āsana, restraint of *prāṇa, dhyāna* and *samādhi* are explained. Again, the nine *cakras* (psychic centers) and the process of meditation on *cakras* are described. Finally, the *Upaniṣad* is completed with a brief account of *cakras*, meditation on *cakras* and their results.

Publisher

ŚĀNTIPĀṬHA

शान्तिपाठः

ॐ सह नाववतु । सह नौ भुनक्तु । सह वीर्यं करवावहै ।

तेजस्विनावधीतमस्तु मा विद्विषावहै ॥

ॐ शान्तिः शान्तिः शान्तिः ॥

oṃ saha nāvavatu /

saha nau bhunaktu /

saha vīryaṃ karavāvahai /

tejasvināvadhītamastu mā vidviṣāvahai /

oṃ śāntiḥ śāntiḥ śāntiḥ //

Om. May He protect both of us together. May He nourish both of us together. May both of us get strength and power together. May our knowledge (given and received between us) be powerful. May there be no animosity between us. Om. May there be peace, peace and peace again in all the three worlds. May the three types of pains/miseries be peaceful.

BOOK FOUR

Yogarāja Upaniṣad

योगराज उपनिषद्

Four Branches of Yoga

योगराजं प्रवक्ष्यामि योगिनां योगसिद्धये ।
मन्त्रयोगो लयश्चैव राजयोगो हठस्तथा ॥१॥

yogarājaṃ pravakṣyāmi yogināṃ yogasiddhaye /
mantrayogo layścaiva rājayogo haṭhastathā //1//

Now *Yogarāja Upaniṣad* is described in order to attain yoga *siddhi* (perfection in yoga) for the yogis. It has four branches of yoga – *mantrayoga, layayoga, rājayoga* and *haṭhayoga.* -1.

योगश्चतुर्विधः प्रोक्तो योगिभिस्तत्त्वदर्शिभिः ।
आसनं प्राणसंरोधो ध्यानं चैव समाधिकः ॥२॥

yogaścaturvidhaḥ prokto yogibhistattvadarśibhiḥ /
āsanaṃ prāṇasamrodho dhyānaṃ caiva samādhikaḥ //2//

Four Types of Yoga

The four limbs of yoga are described by the knowers of the truth of yoga. They are: āsana, restraint of *prāṇa, dhyāna* and *samādhi.* -2.

एतच्चतुष्टयं विद्धि सर्वयोगेषु सम्मतम् ।
ब्रह्मविष्णुशिवादीनां मन्त्रं जाप्यं विशारदैः ॥३॥

etaccatuṣṭayaṃ viddhi sarvayogeṣau saṃatam /
brahmaviṣṇuśivādīnāṃ mantraṃ jāpyaṃ viśāradaiḥ //3//

These four branches of yoga are acknowledged by all (systems/

traditions of) yoga. The wise men should practice the mantras of *Brahmā, Viṣṇu* and *Śivā*. -3.

Mantra Yogis

साध्यते मन्त्रयोगस्तु वत्सराजादिभिर्यथा ।

कृष्णद्वैपायनाद्यैस्तु साधितो लयसंज्ञितः ॥४॥

sādhyate mantrayogastu vatsarājādibhiryathā /

kṛṣṇadvaipāyanāddhyaistu sādhito layasaṅajjñitaḥ //4//

The yogis who perfected *mantrayoga* are *Vatsarāja* and others and *Kṛṣṇadvaipāyana (Vyāsa)* and others attained perfection in the yoga called *Laya*. -4.

Meditation on Nine Cakras

नवस्वेव हि चक्रेषु लयं कृत्वा महात्मभिः ।

प्रथमं ब्रह्मचक्रं स्यात् त्रिरावृत्तं भगाकृति ॥५॥

navasveva hi cakreṣau layaṃ kṛtvā mahātmābhiḥ /

prathamaṃ brahmacakraṃ syāt trirāvṛttaṃ bhagākṛti //5//

The exalted souls attain perfection by dissolving (their minds) into the nine types of *cakras*. The first *cakra* encircled three times is of the shape of *bhaga* (triangle) which is called *brahma cakra*. -5.

Brahma Cakra

अपाने मूलकन्दाख्यं कामरूपं च तज्जगुः ।

तदेव वह्निकुण्डं स्यात् तत्त्वकुण्डलिनी तथा ॥६॥

apāne mūlakandākhyaṃ kāmarūpaṃ ca tajjaguḥ /

tadeva vanhikuṇḍaṃ syāt tattvakuṇḍalinī tathā //6//

Mūlakanda (the bulbous root) in the form of *kāma* is situated at the place of *apāna* which is called *vanhi kuṇḍa* (the lake of fire) and *tattva* (the essence) of *kuṇḍalinī*. -6.

तां जीवरूपिणीं ध्यायेज्ज्योतिष्ठं मुक्तिहेतवे ।

स्वाधिष्ठानं द्वितीयं स्याच्चक्रं तन्मध्यगं विदुः ॥७॥

tāṃ jīvarūpiṇīṃ dhyāyejjyotiṣṭhaṃ muktihetave /

svādhisṭhānaṃ dvitīyaṃ syāccakraṃ tanmadhyagaṃ viduḥ //7//

One should meditate on that light in the form of *jīva* with a desire of liberation. According to the wise men, the second *cakra* called *svādhisṭhāna* is located in the middle of it. -7.

Svādhisṭhāna Cakra

पश्चिमाभिमुखं लिङ्गं प्रवालाङ्कुरसन्निभम् ।

तत्रोद्रीयाणपीठेषु तं ध्यात्वाकर्षयेज्जगत् ॥८॥

paścimābhimukhaṃ liṅgaṃ pravālāṅkurasannibham /

tatrodrīyāṇapīṭheṣu taṃ dhyātvākarṣayejjagat //8//

A *liṅga* facing west is located there having a color of luminous red shoot. At the *udrīyāṇapīṭha* (*svādhisṭhāna cakra*) there one should meditate on that luminous shoot and attract the world. -8.

Nābhi Cakra

तृतीयं नाभिचक्रं स्यात्तन्मध्ये तु जगत् स्थितम् ।

पञ्चावर्तां मध्यशक्तिं चिन्तयेद्विद्युदाकृति ॥९॥

tṛtīyaṃ nābhicakraṃ syāttanmadhye tu jagat sthitam /

pajñcāvartāṃ madhyaśaktiṃ cintayedvidyudākṛti //9//

The third center is the *nābhicakra* (navel center). The world is located in the middle of it. One should meditate on the *Śakti* with the form of shining light in the middle of it. -9.

Hṛdaya Cakra

तां ध्यात्वा सर्वसिद्धीनां भाजनं जायते बुधः ।

चतुर्थे हृदये चक्रं विज्ञेयं तदधोमुखम् ॥१०॥

tām dhyātvā sarvasiddhīnāṃ bhājanaṃ jāyate budhaḥ /

caturthe hṛdaye cakraṃ vijñeyaṃ datadhomukham //10//

A wise person is entitled to attain all kinds of perfections by meditating on it. It should be known that the fourth center *hṛdaya cakra* having its face downward is located at the heart. -10.

ज्योतीरूपं च तन्मध्ये हंसं ध्यायेत् प्रयत्नतः ।

तं ध्यायतो जगत् सर्वं वश्यं स्यान्नात्र संशयः ॥११॥

jyotīrūpaṃ ca tanmadhye haṃsaṃ dhyāyet prayatnataḥ /

taṃ dhyāyato jagat sarvaṃ vaśyaṃ syānnātra samśayaḥ //11//

One should meditate on *haṃsa* in the form of light in the middle of it with due effort. The whole world is subjugated by meditating on it. There should be no doubt about it.

Kaṇṭha Cakra

पञ्चमं कण्ठचक्रं स्यात् तत्र वामे इडा भवेत् ।

दक्षिणे पिङ्गला ज्ञेया सुषुम्ना मध्यतः स्थिता ॥१२॥

pajñcamaṃ kaṇṭhacakraṃ syāt tatra vāme iḍā bhavet /

dakṣiṇe piṅgalā jñeyā suṣaumnā madhyataḥ sthitā //12//

The fifth center is *kaṇṭha cakra* (throat center). It is known that *Iḍā* is located on its left, *piṅgalā* on its right and *suṣaumnā* in the middle of it. -13.

Tālukā Cakra

तत्र ध्यात्वा शुचि ज्योतिः सिद्धीनां भाजनं भवेत् ।

षष्ठं च तालुकाचक्रं घण्टिकास्थानमुच्यते ॥१३॥

tatra dhyātva śuci jyotiḥ siddhinām bhājanaṃ bhavet /

ṣaṣṭhaṃ ca tālukācakraṃ ghaṇṭikāsthānamucyate //13//

By meditating on that Holy Light there (at the *kaṇṭha cakra*) all perfections are attained. The sixth center is *tālukā cakra* (the palate center) which is also called *ghaṇṭikā sthāna*. -14.

दशमद्वारमार्गं तद्राजदन्तं च तज्जगुः ।

तत्र शून्ये लयं कृत्वा मुक्तो भवति निश्चितम् ॥१४॥

daśamadvāramārgaṃ tadrājadantaṃ ca tajjaguḥ /

tatra śūnye layaṃ kṛtvā mukto bhavati niścitam //14//

It is also known as the path of tenth door and *rājadanta* (literally, royal or principal tooth). Having dissolved (his mind) in the void there, a person certainly attains liberation. -14.

Bhrūcakra

भ्रूचक्रं सप्तमं विद्याद्बिन्दुस्थानं च तद्विदुः ।

भ्रुवोर्मध्ये वर्तुलं च ध्यात्वा ज्योतिः प्रमुच्यते ॥ १५॥

bhrūcakraṃ saptaṃ vidyādvindusthānaṃ ca tadviduḥ /

bhruvormadhye vartulaṃ ca dhyātvā jyotiḥ pramucyate //15//

The seventh is the *bhrūcakra* (the eyebrow center). It is called the place of *vidyā* and *vindu.* Yogis attain liberation through meditation on the round shaped light in the middle of the eyebrows. -15.

Brahmarandhra Cakra

अष्टमं ब्रह्मरन्ध्रं स्यात् परं निर्वाणसूचकम् ।

तं ध्यात्वा सूतिकाग्रामं धूमाकारं विमुच्यते ॥१६॥

aṣṭamaṃ brahmarandhraṃ syāt paraṃ nirvāṇasūcakaṃ /

taṃ dhyātvā sūtikāgrāmaṃ dhūmākāraṃ vimucyate //16//

The eighth cakra which is the indicator of supreme liberation is called *brahmarandhra* (the door to *Brahman*). It is said that by meditating on that smoky *sūtikāgrāma* (the source of origin), a yogi attains liberation. -16.

Vyomacakra

तच्च जालन्धरं ज्ञेयं मोक्षदं नीलचेतसम् ।

नवमं व्योमचक्रं स्यादश्रैः षोडशभिर्युतम् ॥१७॥

tacca jālandharaṃ jñeyaṃ mokṣadaṃ nīlacetasam /

navamaṃ vyomacakraṃ syādaśraiḥ ṣaoḍaśabhiryutam //17//

It should be known that the giver of liberation is the dark blue colored *jālandhara.* The ninth cakra which has sixteen petals is called *vyomacakra* (the sky/ether center). -19.

Purṇāgiripīṭha

संविद्ब्रूयाच्च तन्मध्ये शक्तिरुद्धा स्थिता परा ।

तत्र पूर्णां गिरौ पीठे शक्तिं ध्यात्वा विमुच्यते ॥१८॥

samvidbrūyācca tanmadhye śaktiruddhā sthitā parā /

tatra purṇāṃ girau pīṭhe śaktiṃ dhyātvā vimucyate //18//

In the middle of the sixteen petalled lotus the supreme *śakti* is hindered/located which should be called *samvid* (consciousness).

A *sādhaka* attains liberation by meditating on the *purṇāśakti* (the complete power) in the middle of the *purṇāgiripīṭha* (the perfect mountain of pilgrimage). -18.

Results of Cakra Meditation

एतेषां नवचक्राणामेकैकं ध्यायतो मुनेः ।

सिद्धयो मुक्तिसहिताः करस्थाः स्युर्दिने दिने ॥१९॥

eteṣāṃ navacakrāṇāmekaikaṃ dhyāyato muneḥ /

siddhayo muktisahitāḥ karasthāḥ syurdine dine //19//

A yogi who meditates on the above mentioned nine *cakras* one by one in the order (given), he goes on gaining all *siddhis* (perfections) day by day along with liberation. -19.

एको दण्डद्वयं मध्ये पश्यति ज्ञानचक्षुषा ।

कदम्बगोलकाकारं ब्रह्मलोकं व्रजन्ति ते ॥२०॥

eko daṇḍadvayaṃ madhye paśyati jñānacakṣuṣā /

kadambagolakākāraṃ brahmalokaṃ vrajanti te //20//

A *sādhaka* who sees *daṇḍadvaya* (literally, the two sticks) in the middle of the circular *cakra* similar to the *kadamba* blossoms through his eyes of knowledge, he attains the *brahmaloka* (the abode of *Brahma*)

ऊर्ध्वशक्तिनिपातेन अधःशक्तेर्निकुञ्चनात् ।

मध्यशक्तिप्रबोधेन जायते परमं सुखं जायते परमं सुखम् ॥२१॥

ūrdhvaśaktinipātena adhaḥśakternikuñcanāt /

madhyaśktiprabodhena jāyate paraṃ sukhaṃ

jāyate paramaṃ sukham //21//

By descending the upper force and by contracting the lower force and then by raising the middle force a supreme happiness is attained, a supreme happiness is attained.

इति योगराजोपनिषत् समाप्ता ॥

Thus ends the *Yogarāja Upaniṣad*.

शान्तिपाठः

ॐ सह नाववतु । सह नौ भुनक्तु । सह वीर्यं करवावहै ।

तेजस्विनावधीतमस्तु मा विद्विषावहै ॥

ॐ शान्तिः शान्तिः शान्तिः ॥

Śānti Pāṭha

oṃ saha nā-vavatu /

saha nau bhunaktu /

saha vīryaṃ karavāvahai /

tejasvināvadhītamastu mā vidviṣāvahai /

oṃ śāntiḥ śāntiḥ śāntiḥ //

Om. May He protect both of us together. May He nourish both of us together. May both of us get strength and power together. May our knowledge (given and received between us) be powerful. May there be no animosity between us. Om. May there be peace, peace and peace again in all the three worlds. May the three types of pains/miseries be peaceful.

HAṂSA UPANIṢAD

हंस उपनिषद्

Book Five

English Translation Accompanied by Sanskrit

Text in Roman Transliteration

Translated into English by

Swami Vishnuswaroop

Divine Yoga Institute

Kathmandu, Nepal

INTRODUCTION

This *Upaniṣad* belongs to *Sukla Yajurveda.* It is presented in the form of dialogue between *Ṛṣi Gautama* and *Sanatkumāra. Sanatkumāra* imparts the knowledge of *Brahmavidyā* to *Ṛṣi Gautama* which was heard by Goddess *Pārvati* from Lord *Śiva.*

It is said that the mysterious knowledge of *Haṃsa* should be given to one who has has control over his mind and senses and is devoted to his guru. *Haṃsa* in the form of *Jīvātmā* exists in all beings just like the fire in woods and the oil in sesame seeds. The six *cakras* should be penetrated to attain it. The various inclinations of *Haṃsa* are described by the analogy of the eight petalled lotus and the *Brahma* is mentioned as pure like while crystal. *Haṃsa* is a synonymous term for the *Brahma.* It is said that *nāda* is produced by meditating on *Haṃsa.* Thus the various forms of *nāda* are experienced. Realization of *Brahman* is its supreme state. It is also called the state of *samādhi.* The declaration of *Veda* is that the *Brahman* alone shines in that state which is omnipresent, self-radiant, pure and eternal.

Publisher

ŚĀNTIPĀṬHAḤ

शान्तिपाठ:

ॐ पूर्णमदः पूर्णमिदं पूर्णात्पूर्णमुदच्यते ।

पूर्णस्य पूर्णमादाय पूर्णमेवावशिष्यते ॥

ॐ शान्तिः शान्तिः शान्तिः ॥

om pūrṇamadaḥ purṇamidaṃ

pūrṇātpūrṇamudacyate /

pūrṇasya pūrṇamādāya

pūrṇamevāvaśiṣyate //

om śāntiḥ śāntiḥ śāntiḥ //

The Supreme *Brahman*, expressed in the form of OM, is himself Complete (in every way). This whole creation is also complete in itself. This whole world is created from that Complete (Truth). When this whole universe is taken out from that Complete, then the remainder is also Complete. May there be peace in all the three types of suffering.

BOOK FIVE

Haṃsa Upaniṣad

हंस उपनिषद्

Request to Impart Brahma Vidyā

गौतम उवाच ।

भगवन्सर्वधर्मज्ञ सर्वशास्त्रविशारद ।

ब्रह्मविद्याप्रबोधो हि केनोपायेन जायते ॥१॥

gautama uvāca: -

bhagavansarvadharmajña sarvaśāstraviśārada /

brahmavidyāprabodho hi kenopāyena jāyate // 1 //

Ṛṣi Gautama asked *Sanatkumara*: "O Lord! You know all *dharmas* and you have mastered all the *śāstras* (scriptures - *Vedas, Upanishads,* etc.). Please explain me by what means *Brahma Vidyā* (knowledge of the *Brahman*) can be attained. -1.

Means to Brahmavidyā

सनत्कुमार उवाच ।

विचार्य सर्ववेदेषु मतं ज्ञात्वा पिनाकिनः ।

पार्वत्या कथितं तत्त्वं श्रृणु गौतम तन्मम ॥२॥

sanatkumāra uvāca: -

vicārya sarvadharmeṣu mataṃ jñātvā pinākina /

pārvatyā kathitaṃ tattvaṃ śruṇu gautama tanmama //2//

Sanatkumāra replied: - O *Gautama*! Listen attentively. I will explain you what *Pinākina* (Lord *Śiva*) having contemplated on and known all *dharmas* (*Vedas* and *Upaniṣads*) told *Pārvati* about the *Tattva* (Supreme Truth). -2.

Haṃsa Vidyaa Is Mysterious

अनाख्येयमिदं गुह्यं योगिनां कोशसन्निभम् ।

हंसस्याकृतिविस्तारं भुक्तिमुक्तिफलप्रदम् ॥ ३॥

anākhyeyamidaṃ guhyaṃ yogine kośasannibham /

haṃsasyākṛtivistāraṃ bhuktimuktiphalapradam //3//

This great mystery should not be disclosed (to everyone). This is like a treasure of wisdom for yogis. The elegant description of the image of *Haṃsa* (the Supreme Self) bestows both enjoyment (of the *Ātman*) and liberation. -3.

Eligibility for Haṃsa Vidyā

अथ हंसपरमहंसनिर्णयं व्याख्यास्यामः ।

ब्रह्मचारिणे शान्ताय दान्ताय गुरुभक्ताय ।

हंसहंसेति सदा ध्यानम् ॥४॥

atha haṃsaparamahaṃsanirṇayaṃ vyākhyāmaḥ /

brahmacariṇe śāntāya dāntāya gurubhaktāya /

haṃsahaṃseti sadā dhyānam //4//

Now I will explain the conclusion on *Haṃsa* (the Individual *Jīva*) and *Parama Haṃsa* (the Supreme *Ātman*). This mysterious knowledge (of *Haṃsa* and *Parama Haṃsa*) should be imparted to a *brahmacāri* (intently desirous of attaining the *Brahman*) who has equanimous state of mind, subjugated his senses, is devoted to his guru and always meditates on *Haṃsa - Haṃsa* or *Sohaṃ - Sohaṃ*. -4.

Haṃsa Is All Pervasive

सर्वेषु देहेषु व्याप्य वर्तते ॥

यथा ह्यग्निः काष्ठेषु तिलेषु तैलमिव

तं विदित्वा मृत्युमत्येति ॥५॥

sarveṣu deheṣu vyāpto vartate /

yathā hyagniḥ kāṣṭheṣu tileṣu tailamiva

taṃ viditvā mṛtyumatyeti //5//

The *Jīva* (which is always repeating *Haṃsa*) abides in and pervades all beings just like fire exists in every wood and oil in all sesame seeds. Thus, after knowing the *Haṃsa*, one goes beyond death. -5.

Method of Gaining Haṃsa Vidyā

गुदं अवष्टभ्याधारात् वायुमुत्थाप्य स्वाधिष्ठानं
त्रिः प्रदक्षिणीकृत्य मणिपूरकं च गत्वा अनाहतमतिक्रम्य
विशुद्धौ प्राणान्निरुध्या आज्ञामनुध्यायन्ब्रह्मरन्ध्रं ध्यायन्
त्रिमात्रोऽहमित्येव सर्वदा पश्यत्यनाकारश्च भवति ॥६॥

gudaṃ avaṣṭabhyādhārāt vāyumutthāpya svādhiṣṭhānaṃ
triḥ pradakṣinīkṛtya maṇipurakaṃ gattvā anāhatamatikramya
viśuddhau praṇānnirudhya ājñāmanudhyāyan brahmarandhraṃ
dhyāyan trimātro'hamityeva sarvadā paśyatyanākāraśca bhavati //6//

By contracting the perineum the *vāyu* should be raised from the *ādhāra cakra* and it should be made to go around *svādhiṣṭhāna cakra* three times and enter *maṇipura cakra* and penetrate *anāhata cakra.* Then one should restrain the *praṇā* at *viśuddhi cakra* and meditate on *ājñā cakra* and *brahma randhara.* He should meditate on *trimātro'ham* "I am of three *mātrās*" (it is - *saḥ aham* which has three *mātrās* meaning "I am That"). Thus, the yogi always seeing (and contemplating on) the formless *Brahman*, attains the formless state. -6.

एषोऽसौ परमहंसो भानुकोटिप्रतिकाशो सर्वं व्याप्तम् ॥७॥

eṣo'sau paramahṃso bhānukoṭipratikāśo sarvaṃ vyāptam //7//

This *paramahaṃsa* is luminous like the millions of shining suns and the whole universe is pervaded by its light. -7.

The Eight Vṛttis of Haṃsa

तस्याष्टधा वृत्तिर्भवति । पूर्वदले पुण्ये मतिः ।
आग्नेये निद्रालस्यादयो भवन्ति । याम्ये क्रौर्ये मतिः ।
नैर्ऋते पापे मनीषा । वारुण्यां क्रीडा । वायव्ये गमनादौ बुद्धिः ।

सौम्ये रतिप्रीतिः । ईशाने द्रव्यादानम् । मध्ये वैराग्यम् ।
केसरे जाग्रदवस्था । कर्णिकायां स्वप्नम् । लिङ्गे सुषुप्तिः ।
पद्मत्यागे तुरीयम् । यदा हंसो नादे विलीनो भवति
तत् तुरीयातीतम् ॥८॥

tasyāṣṭadhā vṛttirbhavati / pūrvadale puṇye matiḥ /
āgneye nidrālasyādayo bhavanti / yāmye kraurye matiḥ /
nairrhṛte pāpe manīṣā / vāruṇyāṃ krīḍā /
vāyavyāṃ gamanādau buddhiḥ / saumye ratiprītiḥ /
īśānye dravyādānaṃ / madhye vairāgyaṃ /
kesare jāgradavasthā / karṇikāyāṃ svapnaṃ /
liṅge suṣuptiḥ / padmatyāge turīyaṃ /
yadā haṃse nādo vilīno bhavati
tat turīyātītam //8//

This *Haṃsa* has eight types of *vṛttis* (inclinations/ modifications represented by the eight petals of *anāhata cakra*). They are – *puṇya mati* (virtuous thought) in the eastern petal, *nidrā, ālasyādi* (sleep, laziness, etc.) in the southeast petal, *krūra mati* (cruel thought) in the southern petal, *pāpa mana* (wickedness of mind) in the southwestern petal, *krīḍā* (sensual pleasure) in the west petal, *gamana buddhi* (desiring to walk) in the northwest petal, *ratiprīti* (love towards the Self) in the northern petal, *dravyādāna* (donation of wealth) in the northeastern petal, *vairāgya* (detachment) in the middle of the petals, *jāgrat avasthā* (awakened state) in the filament of the lotus, *svapna* (dream state) in the pericarp of the lotus and *suṣupti* (deep sleep) state in *liṅga* (the subtle self). When the *Haṃsa* gives up the *anāhata cakra*, it attains *turīya avasthā* (the fourth state of consciousness). When the *nāda* is absorbed into the *Haṃsa*, then *turīyātīta avasthā* (the state beyond the fourth level of consciousness) is achieved. -8.

Nāda Exists Everywhere

अथो नाद आधाराद्ब्रह्मरन्ध्रपर्यन्तं

शुद्धस्फटिकसङ्काशः ।

स वै ब्रह्म परमात्मेत्युच्यते ॥९॥

atho nāda ādhārādbrahmarandhraparyantaṃ

śuddhasphaṭikasaṅkāśaḥ /

sa vai brahma paramātmetyucyate //9//

In this way the *nāda* exists from the *ādhāra cakra* to *Brahmarandra.* It is the purely bright like a crystal pearl. It is verily called *paramātmā* (the Supreme Self).

Ṛṣi, Chanda, etc. of Nāda

अथ हंस ऋषिः । अव्यक्ता गायत्री छन्दः ।

परमहंसो देवता । अहमिति बीजम् । स इति शक्तिः ।

सोऽहमिति कीलकम् ॥१०॥

atha haṃsa ṛṣiḥ / avyaktā gāyatri chandaḥ /

paramahaṃso devatā / ahamiti bījaṃ / sa iti śaktiḥ /

so'hamiti kīlakam //10//

Thus the *ṛṣi* (of *ajapā* mantra) is *Haṃsa.* Its *chanda* (meter) is *avyakta* (imperceptible) *gāyatri* and *devatā* is *Paramahaṃsa* (the Supreme Soul). *Ham* is *bīja* (seed) mantra and *saḥ* is *śakti* (the energy). *So'ham* is *kīlaka* (the bolt). -10.

Diurnal Repetition of Haṃsa

षट्सङ्ख्यया अहोरात्रयोरेकविंशतिसहस्राणि

षट् शतान्यधिकानि भवन्ति ।

सूर्याय सोमाय निरञ्जनाय निराभासाय

तनु सूक्ष्मं प्रचोदयादिति ॥११॥

अग्नीषोमाभ्यां वौषट् हृदयाद्यङ्गन्यास-

करन्यासौ भवतः ॥१२॥

एवं कृत्वा हृदयेऽष्टदले हंसात्मानं ध्यायेत् ॥१३॥

ṣaṭsaṅkhyayā ahorātrayorekaviṃśatisahasrāṇi

ṣaṭ śatānyadhikāni bhavanti /

sūryāya somāya nirañjanāya nirābhāsāyā-

tanusūkṣma pracodayāditi //11//

agnīṣomābyāṃ vauṣaṭ hṛdayādyaṅganyāsa-

karanyāsau bhavataḥ //12//

evaṃ kṛtvā hṛdaye'ṣṭadale haṃsātmānaṃ dhyāyet //13//

Thus the six numbered aspects (*ṛṣi, chanda, devatā, bīja, śakti* and *kīlaka*) of it (*Haṃsa*) repeat the twenty-one thousands six hundred breaths in a day and night. One should perform *hṛdayādi aṅganyāsa* and *karanyāsa* by repeating this mantra "*sūryāya somāya nirañjanāya nirābhāsāya atanu sūkṣma pracodayāt iti agnīṣomābyāṃ vauṣaṭ*". After doing it, he should contemplate on the *Haṃsa* at the eight petalled lotus (*anāhata cakra*) located in the heart. -11-13.

The Various Aspects of Haṃsa

अग्नीषोमौ पक्षावोङ्कारः शिर उकारो बिन्दु

स्त्रिणेत्रं मुखं रुद्रो रुद्राणी चरणौ ।

द्विविधं कण्ठतः कुर्यादित्युन्मनाः

अजपोपसंहार इत्यभिधीयते ॥१४॥

agnīṣomau pakṣāvoṅkāraḥ śira ukāro bindu

striṇetraṃ mukhaṃ rudro rudrāṇī caraṇau /

dvividhaṃ kaṇṭhataḥ kuryādityunmanāḥ

ajapopasaṃhāra ityabhidhiyate //14//

Agni and *soma* are the two wings/arms (sides/aspects) of the *Haṃsa*, *Oṅkāra* is head, *ukāra* with *bindu* is the third eye, *rudra* is mouth and *rudrāṇī* are the two legs. As per distinction of the qualified and unqualified aspects, one should meditate on *Paramātmā* in the form of *Haṃsa* by producing *nāda* from the throat. *Unmani* state is attained through this practice. This state is called *ajapā upasaṃhāra* (ultimate practice of *ajapājapa*). -14.

एवं हंसवशात्तस्मान्मनो विचार्यते ॥१५॥

evaṃ haṃsavaśāttasmānmano vicāryate //15//

Due to the mind controlled by the *Haṃsa*, consequently, a *sādhaka* constantly contemplates on the *Haṃsa.* -15.

Ten Types of Nāda

अस्यैव जपकोट्यां नादमनुभवति एवं
सर्वं हंसवशान्नादो दशविधो जायते ।
चिणीति प्रथमः । चिञ्चिणीति द्वितीयः ।
घण्टानादस्तृतीयः । शङ्खनादश्चतुर्थकम् ।
पञ्चमस्तन्त्रीनादः । षष्ठस्तालनादः ।
सप्तमो वेणुनादः। अष्टमो मृदङ्गनादः ।
नवमो भेरीनादः । दशमो मेघनादः ॥१६॥
नवमं परित्यज्य दशममेवाभ्यसेत् ॥१७॥

asyaiva japakoṭyāṃ nādamanubhavati evaṃ
sarvaṃ haṃsavaśānnādo daśavidho jāyate /
ciṇīti prathamaḥ / cinciṇīti dvitīyaḥ /
ghaṇṭanādastṛtīyaḥ / śaṅkhanādaścaturtham /
pañcamastantrīnādaḥ / ṣaṣṭhastālanādaḥ /
saptamo veṇunādaḥ / aṣṭamo mṛdaṅganādaḥ /
navamo bherīnādaḥ / daśamo meghanādaḥ //16//
navamaṃ parityajya daśamamevābhyaset //17//

When this (*so'ham*) mantra is repeated ten million times, then one can have the experience of the *nāda*. There are ten types of *nāda* (sound) one can hear when his mind is under the control of *Haṃsa*). The first sound is *ciṇī*, the second *cinciṇī*, the third is the sound of a *ghaṇṭa* (big bell), fourth is the sound of a conch, the fifth is sound of the wire of a harp, the sixth is the sound of cymbals, the seventh is the sound of a flute, the eighth is the sound of a *mṛdaṅga* (drum), the ninth is the sound of a *bherī* (bugle) and the tenth is the thundering sound of clouds. Of these, one should give up the nine *nādas* and verily practice the tenth one. -16-17.

Various Experiences of Nāda

प्रथमे चिञ्चिणीगात्रं द्वितीये गात्रभञ्जनम् ।
तृतीये खेदनं याति चतुर्थे कम्पते शिरः ॥१८॥
पञ्चमे स्रवते तालु षष्ठेऽमृतनिषेवणम् ।
सप्तमे गूढविज्ञानं परा वाचा तथाऽष्टमे ॥१९॥
अदृश्यं नवमे देहं दिव्यं चक्षुस्तथाऽमलम् ।
दशमं परमं ब्रह्म भवेद्ब्रह्मात्मसन्निधौ ॥२०॥

prathame ciñciṇīgātraṃ dvitīye gātrabhañjanam /
tṛtīye svedanaṃ yāti caturthe kampate śiraḥ //18//
pañcame sravate tālu ṣaṣṭhe'mṛtaniṣevaṇam /
saptame gūdkavijñānaṃ parā vācā tathā'ṣṭame //19//
adṛśyaṃ navame dehaṃ divyaṃ cakṣustathā'malam /
daśamaṃ paramaṃ brahma bhavedbrahmātmasannidhau //20//

Tinkling (sensation) is felt in the body by the first *nāda*. Crumbling of the body is felt by the second *nāda*. Sweating is caused by the third *nāda*. Trembling of the head is caused by the fourth *nāda*. Saliva is shed from the palate by the fifth *nāda*. In the sixth *nāda* there is shower of nectar. By the seventh *nāda* the hidden knowledge is attained. By the eighth *nāda* the knowledge of all the scriptures is revealed. Invisibility of the body and clear divine knowledge are gained by the ninth *nāda*. By the tenth *nāda* the knowledge of *Parabrahman* and its realization is accomplished. -18-20.

Result of Dissolution of the Mind in Nāda

तस्मिन्मनो विलीयते मनसि सङ्कल्पविकल्पे
दग्धं पुण्यपापे सदाशिवः शक्त्यात्मा
सर्वत्रावस्थितः स्वयंज्योतिः शुद्धो बुद्धो
नित्यो निरञ्जनः शान्तः प्रकाशत
इति वेदानुवचनं भवतीत्युपनिषत् ॥२१॥

tasminmano vilīyate manasi saṅkalpavikalpe
dagdhaṃ puṇyapāpe sadāśivaḥ śaktyāmā

sarvatrāvasthitaḥ svayamjyotiḥ śuddho

buddho nityo nirañjanaḥ śāntaḥ prakaśata

iti vedānuvachanaṃ bhavatītypaniṣat //21//

When the mind is dissolved in *Paramātmā* in the form of *Haṃsa*, volition and doubt in the mind get dissolved and virtue and vice are also burnt down. Then the *Haṃsa* as *Ātman* in the form of *Śiva* and *Śakti* (intelligence) always shines and exists omnipresent, self-radiant, pure and enlightened, eternal and pristine, peaceful and luminous. So is the declaration of *Veda.* Thus ends the *upaniṣat.* -21.

शान्तिपाठ:

ॐ पूर्णमद: पूर्णमिदं पूर्णात्पूर्णमुदच्यते ।

पूर्णस्य पूर्णमादाय पूर्णमेवावशिष्यते ॥

ॐ शान्तिः शान्तिः शान्तिः ॥

śānti pāṭha

om pūrṇamadaḥ purṇamidaṃ

pūrṇātpūrṇamudacyate /

pūrṇasya pūrṇamādāya

pūrṇamevāvaśiṣyate //

om śāntiḥ śāntiḥ śāntiḥ //

The Supreme Brahman, expressed in the form of OM, is himself Complete (in every way). This whole creation is also complete in itself. This whole world is created from that Complete (Truth). When this whole universe is taken out from that Complete, then the remainder is also Complete. May there be peace in all the three types of suffering.

A KEY TO TRANSLITERATION

Vowels

अ आ इ ई उ ऊ ऋ ॠ

a ā i ī u ū ṛ ṝ

ऌ ॡ ए ऐ ओ औ अं अः

lṛ lṝ e ai o au aṃ aḥ

Consonants

क ख ग घ ङ - Gutturals:

ka kha ga gha ṅa

च छ ज झ ञ - Palatals:

ca cha ja jha ña

ट ठ ड ढ ण - Cerebrals:

ṭa ṭha ḍa ḍha ṇa

त थ द ध न - Dentals:

ta tha da dha na

प फ ब भ म - Labials:

pa pha ba bha ma

य र ल व - Semivowels:

ya ra la va

श ष स ह - Sibilants:

śa ṣa sa ha

क्ष त्र ज्ञ - Compound Letters:

kṣa tra jña

Aspirate: ह - ha, Anusvara: अं - aṃ

Visharga - aḥ - अः

Unpronounced अ - a - ऽ - ’, आ - ā - ऽऽ - ”

ALSO BY THIS AUTHOR

Yoga Kundalini Upanishad (in English)
Yoga Darshana Upanishad (in English)
Minor Yoga Upanishads (in English)
Hatha Yoga Pradipoka (in English)
Yogatattva Upanishad (in English)
Two Yoga Samhitas (in English)
Triyoga Upanishad (in English)
Gheranda Samhita (in English)
Goraksha Samhita (in English)
Surya Namskara (in Nepali)
Shiva Samhita (in English)
Shiva Samhita (in Nepali)
Durga Strotram (in Nepali)
Vagalamukhi Stotram (in Nepali)
Amogha Shivakavacham (in Nepali)

ABOUT THE AUTHOR

Swami Vishnuswaroop (Thakur Krishna Uprety), B. A. (Majored in English & Economics), received his Diploma in Yogic Studies (First Class) from Bihar Yoga Bharati, Munger, Bihar, India. He was formally trained under the direct guidance and supervision of Swami Niranjanananda Saraswati in the Guru Kula tradition of the Bihar School of Yoga. He was initiated into the lineage of Swami Satyananda Saraswati, the founder of Bihar School of Yoga and the direct disciple of Swami Sivananda Saraswati of Rishikesh. His guru gave his spiritual name 'Vishnuswaroop' while he was initiated into the sannyasa tradition.

Divine Yoga Institute has published his nine books on classical yoga, meditation and tantra. He is one of the few yoga practitioners registered with Nepal Health Professional Council established by The Government of Nepal. He has been teaching on the theory and practice of traditional yoga and the yogic way of life to Nepalese and foreign nationals for more than twenty-five years.

Swami Vishnuswaroop has designed a comprehensive yoga program called 'Yoga Passport' in order to give a broader theoretical and practical knowledge of yoga which includes various aspects of yogic practice. Many health professionals, yoga practitioners and people from various backgrounds of more than forty-seven countries from various parts of the world have gone through his yoga courses and programs. He currently works as the

President of Divine Yoga Institute, Kathmandu, Nepal and travels abroad to provide yogic teaching and training.

ABOUT THE PUBLISHER

Divine Yoga Institute, which follows Satyananda Yoga tradition, offers a wide variety of group and individual courses in Yogic art and science. Classes at the Institute contribute to the development of a healthy body, a healthy mind, and healthy thought. Institute teachers help students achieve balanced, harmonious and integrated development of all the aspects of their personalities.

The goal of the Divine Yoga Institute is to promote a Yogic system of life with Yoga as a pathway to true, happy, and healthy living. Yogic training eventually prepares one for spiritual awakening, the supreme aim of human life. Keeping in view of this fact objective Divine Yoga Institute has published nine books on classical yoga, meditation and tantra authored and translated by Swami Vishnuswaroop.

Divine Yoga Institute has published his nine books on classical yoga, meditation and tantra. He is one of the few yoga practitioners registered with Nepal Health Professional Council established by The Government of Nepal. He has been teaching on the theory and practice of traditional yoga and the yogic way of life to Nepalese and foreign nationals for more than twenty-five years.

Divine Yoga Institute was established in 1998 by a team of qualified Yoga professionals who received their academic degrees from Bihar Yoga Bharati (BYB) in the *Guru Kula* tradition of Bihar School of Yoga (BSY), Munger, India. BYB is the first Yoga Institute for advanced yogic studies of its kind in the world. Divine Yoga Institute follows the BSY/BYB method of teaching, founded by *Swami Satyananda Saraswati*, a direct disciple of *Swami Shivananda Saraswati* of Rishikesh. *Swami Satyananda* promoted the most profound and holistic aspects of Yoga, covering body, mind, emotions, intellect, spirit and karma. He was the first to widely popularize and spread the therapeutic effects of Yoga.

Made in the USA
Middletown, DE
01 December 2023

43951131R00045